iMath
Readers

Start the Game:
Geometry in Sports

by John Perritano

Content Consultant
David T. Hughes
Mathematics Curriculum Specialist

NORWOOD HOUSE PRESS
Chicago, IL

Norwood House Press
PO Box 316598
Chicago, IL 60631

For information regarding Norwood House Press, please visit our website at
www.norwoodhousepress.com or call 866-565-2900.

Special thanks to: Heidi Doyle
Production Management: Six Red Marbles
Editors: Linda Bullock and Kendra Muntz
Printed in Heshan City, Guangdong, China. 208N—012013

Library of Congress Control Number: 2012949927

ISBN: 978-1-59953-563-0

Summary: The mathematical concept of identifying shapes based upon their
attributes is introduced as readers learn about plane shapes in different sports.
Readers learn how line segments, angles, and special attributes can help to name
geometric shapes. This book includes a discovery activity, a connection to
history, and a mathematical vocabulary introduction.

CONTENTS

Note to Caregivers:

Throughout this book, many questions are posed to the reader. Some are open-ended and ask what the reader thinks. Discuss these questions with your child and guide him or her in thinking through the possible answers and outcomes. There are also questions posed which have a specific answer. Encourage your child to read through the text to determine the correct answer. Most importantly, encourage answers grounded in reality while also allowing imaginations to soar. Information to help support you as you share the book with your child is provided in the back in the **Additional Notes** section.

Bold words are defined in the glossary in the back of the book.

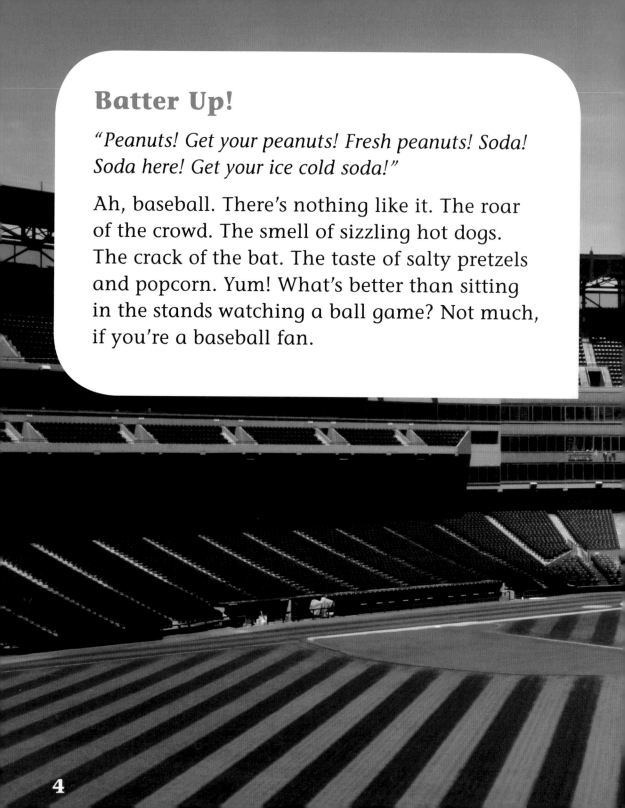

Batter Up!

"Peanuts! Get your peanuts! Fresh peanuts! Soda! Soda here! Get your ice cold soda!"

Ah, baseball. There's nothing like it. The roar of the crowd. The smell of sizzling hot dogs. The crack of the bat. The taste of salty pretzels and popcorn. Yum! What's better than sitting in the stands watching a ball game? Not much, if you're a baseball fan.

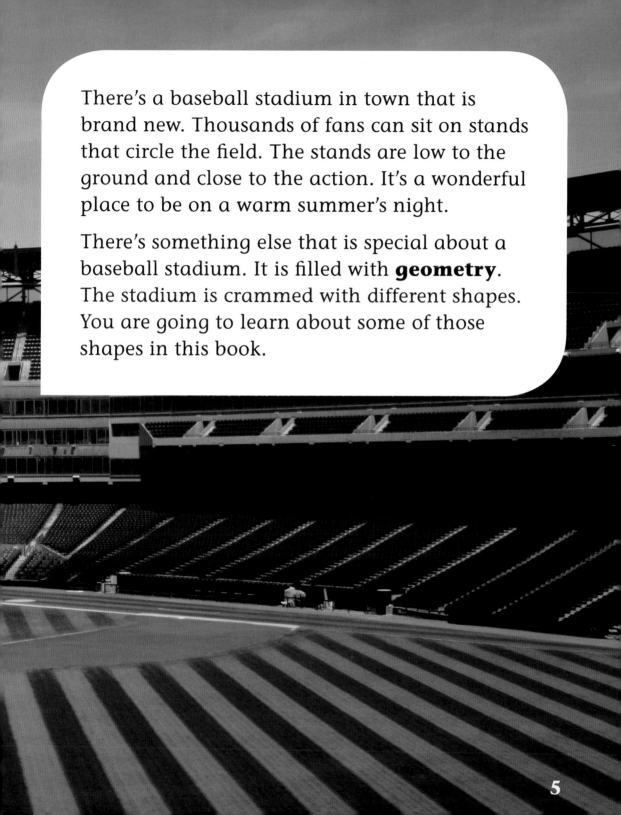

There's a baseball stadium in town that is brand new. Thousands of fans can sit on stands that circle the field. The stands are low to the ground and close to the action. It's a wonderful place to be on a warm summer's night.

There's something else that is special about a baseball stadium. It is filled with **geometry**. The stadium is crammed with different shapes. You are going to learn about some of those shapes in this book.

A baseball field has two fields, an infield and an outfield. The infield is the center of action. It's where home plate and the pitcher's mound are. First, second, and third base are also part of the infield.

An infield is a **plane figure**. A plane figure has length and width. But it has no thickness. It is flat. **Polygons** are plane figures. They have three or more straight sides. They are alike in some ways, and different in others. The things that make each kind of polygon special are called its **attributes**. Attributes are the characteristics that things have.

Sports and the places they are played are filled with polygons. Next time you go to a game, see what polygons you can find.

Look around. Polygons are everywhere. You can use their attributes to help identify them. How?

Idea 1: You can **count sides** to name shapes. The number of sides a shape has is an attribute. Look at the examples in the chart.

3 sides	Triangle	
4 sides	Quadrilateral	
5 sides	Pentagon	
6 sides	Hexagon	
7 sides	Heptagon	
8 sides	Octagon	

Idea 2: You can **use angles** to identify shapes. An **angle** is two **rays**, or parts of a line, that share an endpoint, or **vertex**. A vertex is a point where two rays meet.

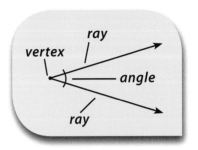

You can also think of an angle as a turn around a point. For example, Earth makes one complete turn, or moves 360°, in 24 hours. Some turns are less than 90°. Others are greater than 90°. Angles that turn exactly 90° are called **right angles**.

Acute Triangle	Obtuse Triangle	Right Triangle
Each angle measures less than 90°.	One angle measures greater than 90°.	One angle measures 90°.

Idea 3: You can also **use the lengths of sides** to identify shapes.

Isosceles Triangle	Equilateral Triangle	Scalene Triangle
Two sides are the same length.	All three sides are the same length.	No sides are the same length.

Idea 4: You can **look for special attributes** to identify **quadrilaterals**. Quadrilaterals are polygons with four sides. They have other attributes, too. Look at the examples in the chart.

Name	Side Attributes	Angle Attributes
Trapezoid	One pair of sides is parallel. The other pair is not.	No angles need to be congruent, or have the same measure.
Parallelogram	Both pairs of sides are parallel. Each pair of parallel sides is of equal length.	The opposite angles of a parallelogram are the same size.
Kite	The sides marked with one line are of equal length. So are the sides marked with two lines.	The angles between the unequal sides are the same size.
Rhombus	All sides are of equal length.	A rhombus has no right angles.
Square	All sides are of equal length.	A square has four right angles.
Rectangle	Parallel sides are of equal length.	A rectangle has four right angles.

DISCOVER ACTIVITY

Materials
- paper
- pencil

It's Plane to See

Look for plane shapes inside your house. You're sure to find them.

Draw a chart like the one below. Leave lots of room to name what you find. There are examples in the chart and photo below.

Room	Object	Geometric Shape
Kitchen	a. Soccer ball magnet b. Paper	a. The magnet is a circle. There are hexagons on the soccer ball design. b. The paper is a rectangle.

Look in several rooms. Look on the walls, floors, and ceilings. Look at furniture. Record what objects you find and where you find them. Then, identify each object's geometric shape.

Now, make a new chart. This time, look for shapes outside. The shapes might be on a playground or in a park. They might be in a garden or on a city street.

Location	Object	Geometric Shape
School playground	Hopscotch game	Squares

Record what you find and where you find it. Then, identify each object's geometric shape.

Going, Going, Gone

The Brown Sox are the hometown team, and they are up to bat. The bases are loaded with runners waiting for a chance to score. And score they must. The score is 4–0, with the visiting Whirlybirds in the lead.

The bases are full. José Rodriguez looks Whirlybird pitcher Johnny Blanton in the eye. One more ball will let Rodriquez walk to first. The player on 3rd base will come home to score. One more strike, and the game will be over.

Blanton pitches the ball. Rodriguez takes a mighty swing. The ball explodes from his bat. It flies into the air. It soars. It's going, going, gone! It's a home run. But it is no ordinary home run. It is a **grand slam**. That's a home run that happens when the bases are full.

The bases are equal distances apart around the infield. Each base is 90 feet from the next, and at a right angle. That forms a square. It's called a baseball diamond.

Rodriquez's grand slam gave all of the players waiting on the bases a chance to score. They reached home plate one at a time, followed by Rodriguez.

Home plate is the most important part of any baseball diamond. A player's body must touch home plate for the player to score a run. The players in this inning tied the score. Both teams had 4 runs.

Two batters after Rodriguez, there was another home run. This time, Nick Parent brought another player and himself across home plate. That changed the score to 6–4, and won the game for the Brown Sox.

Look at the picture of home plate below.

1. How many sides does home plate have?

2. What shape is home plate?

3. How many right angles does home plate have?

Math at Work

Who's the most important person on a major league baseball field? The pitcher? The catcher? The manager? No. It's the groundskeeper. There is no baseball field without a groundskeeper.

A groundskeeper cares for every part of the baseball field. Sometimes, it takes a team of groundskeepers to keep a field in perfect shape.

Groundskeepers must understand geometry to do their jobs. There are rules for distances and shapes on all baseball fields. For example, a major league baseball field has two boxes on either side of home plate. These are the batters' boxes. There is one for right-handed batters and one for left-handed batters. Each box is a rectangle that measures 4 feet by 6 feet. The catcher's box is between the batters' boxes and behind home plate. This box measures 8 feet long and 43 inches wide.

Imagine two rays with home plate as a shared endpoint. One ray goes to 1st base. The other goes to 3rd base. The angle between them measures 90°. What kind of angle is this?

The lines to 1st and 3rd bases are base foul lines. A ball outside those lines is a **foul ball**.

A baseball field includes two boxes for the teams' coaches. One is near 1st base, and the other is near 3rd base. Both boxes are rectangles that must be exactly 8 feet away from the base foul lines.

Measuring shapes and distances is an important job for groundskeepers. So are mowing the grass, keeping the playing field level, and shaping the pitcher's mound.

Football Frenzy

Baseball isn't the only sport with lots of fans. It isn't the only sport with lots of geometry either.

For many sports fans, football is the game of choice. American-style football was born in 1879. That's when the game's first rules were written.

The fans at this game are cheering for a university team.

People around the world know what a football field looks like. Yet, it's only a simple quadrilateral.

The entire field is 360 feet long and 160 feet wide. It is divided into three smaller rectangles. The largest of these three is in the center of the field. It's the playing field. The rectangles on the end are called **end zones**.

The playing field is where the action happens. Players try to move a ball into an end zone. That's where they score points.

The playing field is 100 yards long and $53\frac{1}{3}$ yards wide. White lines surround this rectangle. A player who carries the ball across one of those lines is out of bounds. That stops the play. The player cannot move the ball toward the end zone.

Look at the diagram of a football field below. It shows **line segments**, or parts of lines. It also labels the vertices, or points where line segments meet.

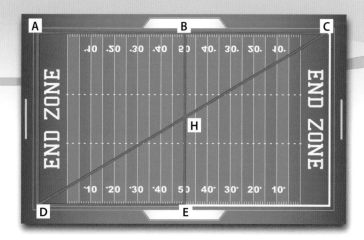

1. Which line segment goes down the center of the football field?
2. Use vertices to identify a trapezoid in the diagram.
3. Use vertices to identify a rectangle in the diagram.
4. Which vertices identify the right triangles in the diagram?

King Edward III was unhappy with his soldiers. They spent too much time on the football field.

Connecting to History

Most people say that England is the birthplace of soccer. In the 1300s, the sport was violent. Players were allowed to kick, punch, and bite. The game was so popular that many people stayed around the field all day to watch. Some stories say that even soldiers stopped training to watch or play the game.

Finally, King Edward III said, "Enough!" He banned soccer in England in 1365. The game, he thought, was too violent. And soldiers were spending too much time away from their work.

But the game didn't go away. In the 1800s, people wrote new rules for two kinds of football. In rugby, players could carry the ball and trip other players. But in soccer, players had to keep their hands off the ball. And they weren't allowed to trip or elbow other players.

Bend It Like Beckham

It was soccer at its best. The date was October 6, 2001. England was playing Greece for a place in the World Cup, the "Super Bowl" of soccer. An action by the Greek team gave the English team a free kick. England's David Beckham took the kick.

Beckham placed the ball at a right angle about 89 feet from the goal. He walked away. Then, he ran toward the ball. He kicked the ball slightly off center. The ball spun, and spun, and spun. It soared over the heads of the Greek players. As it soared, the ball turned left and slowed. It dipped into the goal. The crowd went wild.

The kick thrilled fans. In no time, people began to use the expression "Bend it like Beckham" to describe the ball's movement. The kick was so amazing that scientists from around the world studied films of the kick to understand how it happened.

David Beckham can make a soccer ball turn and dip.

Today, soccer is popular around the world. Perhaps you play soccer. If so, you know what a soccer field looks like.

A modern soccer field is filled with geometric figures. Look at the diagram of a soccer field below.

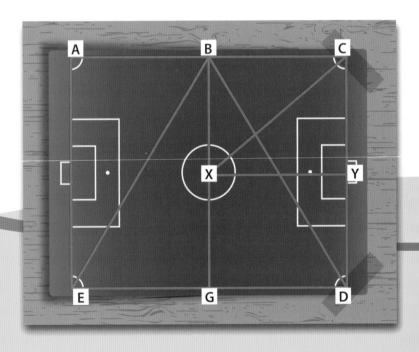

1. What kind of triangle do the line segments *BD*, *DG*, and *GB* form?
2. In the diagram, the line segments *BE*, *ED*, and *DB* are the same length. What kind of triangle do they form?
3. What kind of angle is ∠*BGE*?
4. What kind of angle is ∠*AEB*?
5. Which shape does the line segment *XC* cut in half?

Push It Forward

Baseball, football, and soccer are team sports. But some athletes play alone. One of those players is the shot putter.

The shot put is a throwing event. Players use one hand to throw a heavy metal ball called a **shot**. Adult players use shots that weigh from about 9 to 16 pounds.

This player is getting ready to throw a shot put.

A shot putter starts a throw from inside a circle. She tucks the shot under her chin. Then, she spins several times to gain speed. Finally, she pushes the shot forward. She must push the shot above shoulder height.

A shot putter wants to push a shot forward at an angle of less than 40°. What kind of angle is this?

Shuffle Off

Not all sports require players to throw a heavy metal ball. Take shuffleboard, for example.

Shuffleboard began in England in the 1600s. It was an indoor game. Players shoved coins called "groats" from one side of a table to the other. The winner was the player whose coin stopped closest to the table's edge.

Today, players use pucks like these to play shuffleboard.

In time, players played with silver pennies instead of groats. They started to call the game "shove penny" and "shovel board." Today, the game is called "shuffleboard," and players use pucks instead of pennies.

In the 1800s, ship owners looked for ways to entertain passengers on sea voyages. A ship employee designed a shuffleboard court on the deck of a ship. Instead of coins, players used disks. And instead of shoving the disks, players used long sticks to push the disks across the court.

The first shuffleboard court on land appeared in Daytona Beach, Florida, in 1913. Soon, there were more courts and even shuffleboard clubs. Today, six countries, including the United States and Canada, have national shuffleboard organizations.

Look at the picture of an outdoor shuffleboard court.

1. Where do you see some triangles?

2. Where do you see some trapezoids?

3. Look at the shape marked with the word "OFF." Name the three kinds of angles inside the shape.

Cue Up!

Pool is a **cue sport**. It requires a stick, called a cue stick, some hard balls, and a table shaped like a rectangle. It also requires players to know a lot about angles.

Angles are important in cue sports. Players want to hit a cue ball at just the right angle. This will cause the cue ball to hit a second ball in exactly the right spot. This hit pushes the second ball into one of the pockets around the table.

A good pool player knows how to hit a ball to make it bounce back at a certain angle.

The sides of a pool table are called the rails. Sometimes players strike a ball off the rail. The ball hits the rail at an angle. Then, it bounces off of the rail at the same angle. Look at the picture of a pool table below.

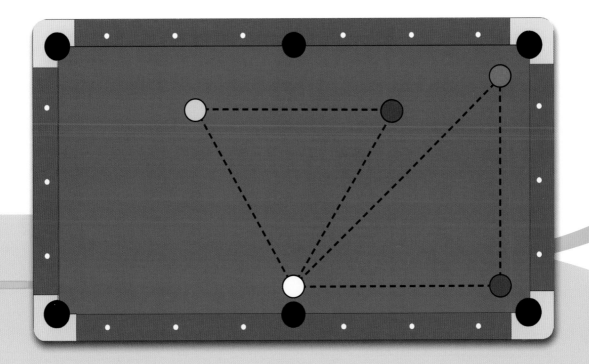

1. Look at the triangle formed by the white, red, and green balls. What kind of triangle is it?

2. What kinds of angles are inside the triangle formed by the white, red, and green balls?

3. Look at the triangle formed by the white, yellow, and blue balls. Say each side is equal in length. What kind of triangle is it?

Come Sail Away

Some sailors sail racing ships called yachts. The America's Cup is the world's most famous yacht race. It began in 1851. That's when an American ship sailed past Queen Victoria's royal yacht. Queen Victoria was watching a sailing race at the time. She asked about the ship and its crew. The ship was a **schooner** called *America*. The crew were members of the New York Yacht Club.

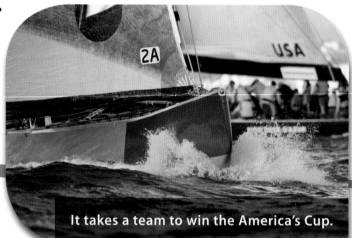

It takes a team to win the America's Cup.

America won the race and the **trophy**, a cup. The people who owned the schooner sold it. And they gave the trophy to the New York Yacht Club. The trophy led to a new race that would be held every year for sailors around the world. The race was named after the schooner. It was called the America's Cup.

Some say that the America's Cup is the most difficult trophy sport in the world. Only four countries have won the cup in more than 150 years of racing.

iMath *IDEAS:* *Sailing Shapes*

A schooner is a different kind of ship. It has at least two masts. One is taller than the other. Each mast rises up from the ship's deck. It supports a ship's sails and rigging. The rigging is the collection of chains and ropes that sailors use to raise and lower sails.

Look at the photograph below of sailors climbing a schooner's rigging. Can you see the polygons?

Would you like to climb rigging to sail a ship?

Look at the drawing of a schooner below. The drawing has many polygons. How can you identify them?

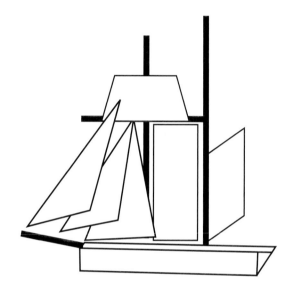

Idea 1: You can **count the sides** of a shape to identify shapes.

Idea 2: You can **use angles** to identify shapes.

Idea 3: You can **use side lengths** to identify shapes.

Idea 4: You can **look for special attributes** to identify quadrilaterals.

What polygons can you identify on this schooner?

Sail a schooner. Pitch a baseball. Catch a football. Sit in a stadium. No matter what sport you play or watch, you will see polygons everywhere.

WHAT COMES NEXT?

Sailing flags have meanings. One flag, for example, tells sailors that a race is about to begin. A different flag tells sailors to come back to the start. And another flag warns sailors to wear life vests.

Sailing flags use a combination of polygons. The polygons are usually red, blue, black, yellow, and white.

Think of some messages you could communicate with flags. Write the messages. Then, design a flag for each one. Decide which shapes and colors show each message the best.

Use colored paper or colored pens to design a set of personal flags. Share the flags with friends and explain their meanings. Invite your friends to make their own flags so that you can communicate with each other.

GLOSSARY

angle: two rays that share an endpoint.

attributes: similar qualities or characteristics.

cue sport: any sport that uses a cue stick. Pool and billiards are cue sports.

end zones: 10-yard areas on opposite ends of a football field.

foul ball: a baseball that travels outside the first and third base lines into an area called foul territory.

geometry: the area of mathematics that deals with points, lines, shapes, and space.

grand slam: a home run hit when all of the bases are loaded. All of the players run to home plate and score one run each.

line segment(s): a part of a line between two endpoints.

plane figure: a flat figure that has length and width but no thickness.

polygons: shapes with three or more straight sides.

quadrilateral(s): polygons with four sides.

ray(s): one arm of an angle.

right angle(s): an angle that turns 90° around a point.

schooner: a ship with two masts, or poles, from which the sails hang.

shot: a metal sphere used in the sport shot put.

trophy: an award or object that recognizes a special achievement.

vertex (vertices): points at which two lines, line segments, or rays meet.

FURTHER READING

FICTION
Mummy Math: An Adventure in Geometry, by Cindy Neuschwander, Square Fish 2009

NONFICTION
Baseball: How it Works, by David Louis Dreier, Sports Illustrated for Kids, 2010
Lines, Segments, Rays, and Angles, by Claire Piddock, Crabtree Publishing Company, 2011

ADDITIONAL NOTES

The page references below provide answers to questions asked throughout the book. Questions whose answers will vary are not addressed.

Page 13: 1. five; 2. pentagon; 3. two right angles

Page 15: right angle

Page 17: 1. line segment *BE*; 2. trapezoid *ABHD*; 3. rectangle *ABED*; 4. right triangle *DEH*, right triangle *ADC,* and right triangle *HBC*

Page 20: 1. right triangle; 2. equilateral triangle; 3. right angle; 4. acute angle; 5. rectangle

Page 21: acute angle

Page 23: 1. Some triangle examples include: Section 10 at the top of the court is a triangle. Together, the sections marked 8, 8, and 10 make a triangle.
So do the sections marked 7, 7, 8, 8, and 10. 2. Some trapezoid examples include: Sections 10, OFF, 7, 7, 8, and 8 are each trapezoids. Together, sections 8 and 8 make a trapezoid. Together, sections 7 and 7 make a trapezoid. Together, sections 10 and OFF on the bottom make a trapezoid. 3. There are two right angles, one obtuse angle, and one acute angle.

Page 25: 1. right triangle; 2. two acute angles and one right angle; 3. equilateral triangle

Page 28: Answers may include triangles, rectangles, parallelograms, and trapezoids.

INDEX

CONTENT CONSULTANT

David T. Hughes

David is an experienced mathematics teacher, writer, presenter, and adviser. He serves as a consultant for the Partnership for Assessment of Readiness for College and Careers. David has also worked as the Senior Program Coordinator for the Charles A. Dana Center at The University of Texas at Austin and was an editor and contributor for the *Mathematics Standards in the Classroom* series.